To

From

Date

A STILL AND QUIET PLACE

HOPE LYDA

Paintings by DARRELL BUSH

HARVEST HOUSE PUBLISHERS

EUGENE, OREGON

In loving memory of my uncle Wally Bowman—
a man of faith, prayer, and great kindness.

HOPE LYDA

A Still and Quiet Place

Published by Harvest House Publishers
Eugene, Oregon 97402
www.harvesthousepublishers.com

ISBN 978-0-7369-4234-8

Design and production by Garborg Design Works, Savage, Minnesota

Harvest House Publishers has made every effort to trace the ownership of all poems and quotes. In the event of a question arising from the use of a poem or quote, we regret any error made and will be pleased to make the necessary correction in future editions of this book.

All Scripture quotations are taken from the *Holy Bible, New International Version® NIV®*. Copyright © 1973, 1978, 1984, 2011 by Biblica, Inc.™ Used by permission. All rights reserved worldwide.

Printed in China

12 13 14 15 16 17 18 19 20 /FC / 10 9 8 7 6 5 4 3 2 1

The further the soul is from the noise of the world, the closer it may be to its Creator, for God, with his holy angels, will draw close to a person who seeks solitude and silence.

THOMAS À KEMPIS

CONTENTS

YOU'RE INVITED

*I*t's time to take a mini vacation. Don't concern yourself with packing. In fact, you're asked to leave your baggage behind. Everything you need will be given to you. This is your much-needed, well-deserved getaway, compliments of Creation.

There's a path that leads to the still and quiet place just up ahead. The trailhead is marked with a crooked sign planted among an inviting patch of sunflowers. This is your engraved invitation to the peaceful life. Lean in close, and you can read its instructions...

Whatever is true,
whatever is noble,
whatever is right,
whatever is pure,
whatever is lovely,
whatever is admirable
—if anything is excellent
or praiseworthy—
think about such things.

PHILIPPIANS 4:8

The foolish man seeks happiness in the distance; the wise grows it under his feet.

JAMES OPPENHEIM

Relax. Take a deep breath. Have a seat wherever you'd like: on the porch swing, the red chair on the dock, the small stretch of beach where the river turns. The journey to the refuge of stillness is one of the heart and mind, and Creation's beauty is the best map of all.

Is it so small a thing
To have enjoyed the sun,
To have lived light in the spring,
To have loved, to have thought, to have done?

MATTHEW ARNOLD

We do not see
nature with our
eyes, but with our
understandings
and our hearts.

WILLIAM HAZLITT

I loaf and invite my soul.

WALT WHITMAN

You make known to me the path of life;
you will fill me with joy in your presence.

Psalm 16:11

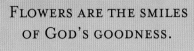

FLOWERS ARE THE SMILES
OF GOD'S GOODNESS.

WILLIAM WILBERFORCE

Happiness resides not in possessions and not in gold;

the feeling of happiness dwells in the soul.

DEMOCRITUS

Flowers are God's thoughts of beauty, taking form to gladden mortal gaze; bright gems of earth, in which, perchance, we see what Eden was—what Paradise may be!

AUTHOR UNKNOWN

The glow of inspiration warms us; this holy rapture springs from the seeds of the Divine mind sown in man.

OVID

9

As the deer pants for streams of water,
so my soul pants for you, my God.
My soul thirsts for God, for the living God.
When can I go and meet with God?

PSALM 42:1-2

Adopt the pace of nature:
her secret is patience.

RALPH WALDO EMERSON

*The contemplative
life must provide
an area, a space of
liberty, of silence, in
which possibilities
are allowed to
surface and new
choices—beyond
routine choice—
become manifest.*

THOMAS MERTON

A lake carries you into recesses of feeling otherwise impenetrable.

WILLIAM WORDSWORTH

WHATEVER IS TRUE AND NOBLE

*W*hen you first stumble across a physical place or an emotional space draped in silence and beauty, you might feel as though you have, like Alice in Wonderland, left reality and entered a new world. But, oh how lucky you are! This is not an imaginary realm. It is the very real home of the deepest truth. In the absence of clatter from yesterday's worries and tomorrow's what-ifs, the stillness can be startling. But slowly, the silence gives way to the sweet, lively soundtrack of birdcalls and the jubilant hollers of water rushing and tumbling over layers of stone.

You feel a momentum for the first time in days, weeks, months! But you aren't sure if you are prepared for the adventure of peace. As scout leaders, camp lifeguards, daycare workers—and God—all know, the buddy system is the best way to embark on adventures, including internal ones. Your buddy is that still, small voice that has been with you from the very beginning. And when you pay attention, it is the encourager who helps you become your noble, true self in triumph and trial alike.

Unsure of the way to go? Look around you. There's a majestic thousand-year-old redwood claiming a portion of the sky. There's a boulder, shiny from years of being polished by the elements and perhaps even by the steps of many other solace seekers. Strength and endurance are illuminated all around you. Leave falseness behind. Press on and let integrity and authenticity become trustworthy stepping-stones toward the unmatched bliss of intentional living. Off you go.

All seasons are beautiful for the person who carries happiness within.

HORACE FRIESS

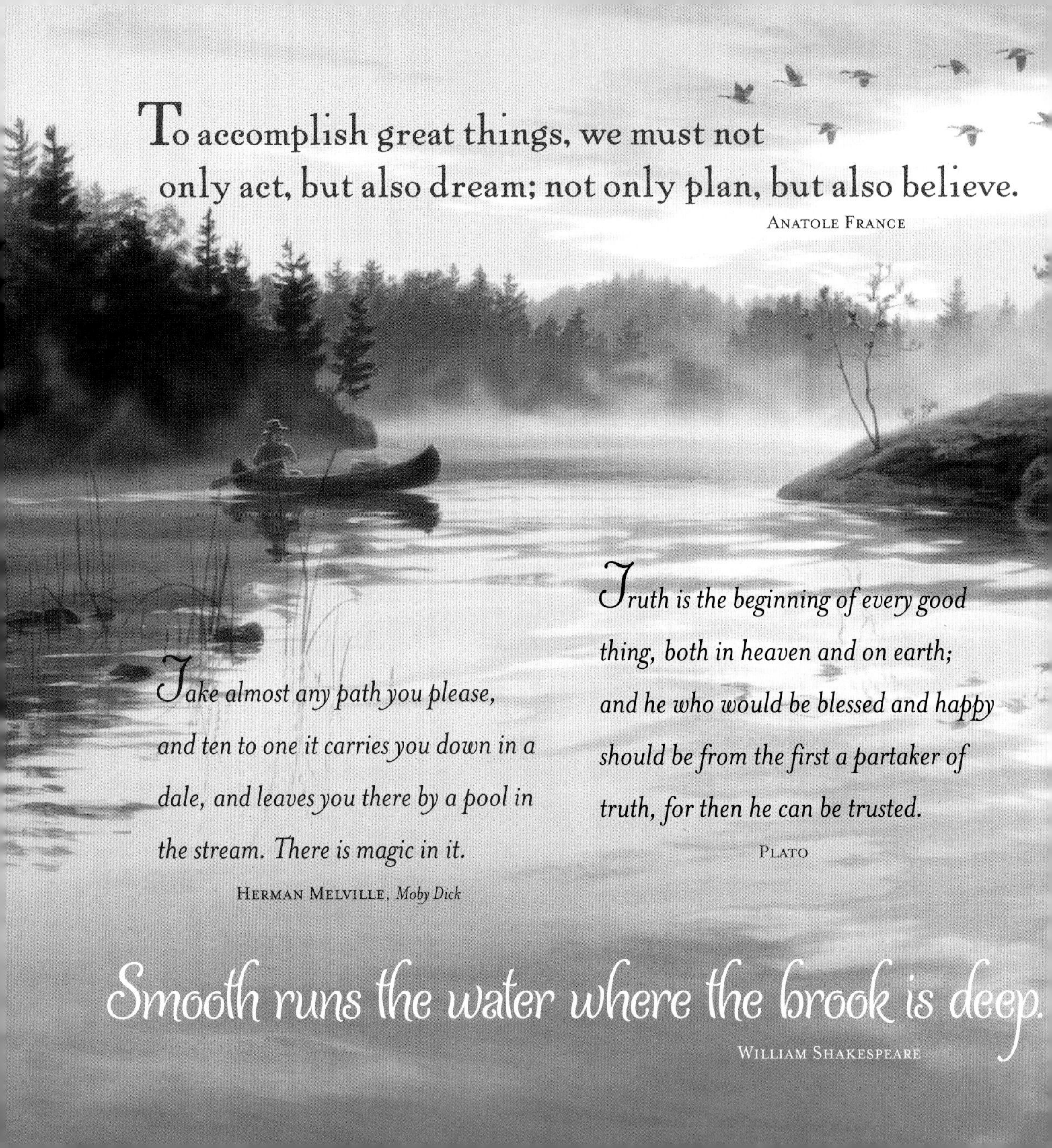

To accomplish great things, we must not only act, but also dream; not only plan, but also believe.

ANATOLE FRANCE

Take almost any path you please, and ten to one it carries you down in a dale, and leaves you there by a pool in the stream. There is magic in it.

HERMAN MELVILLE, *Moby Dick*

Truth is the beginning of every good thing, both in heaven and on earth; and he who would be blessed and happy should be from the first a partaker of truth, for then he can be trusted.

PLATO

Smooth runs the water where the brook is deep.

WILLIAM SHAKESPEARE

IT IS A SPLENDID THING TO HAVE THE USE OF ANY
GIFT OF GOD. IT ISN'T FOR US TO CHOOSE AGAIN,
OR WONDER AND DISPUTE, BUT JUST WORK IN OUR
OWN PLACES, AND LEAVE THE REST TO GOD.

SARAH ORNE JEWETT

I HEAR LAKE WATER
LAPPING WITH LOW
SOUNDS BY THE SHORE...
I HEAR IT IN THE DEEP
HEART'S CORE.

WILLIAM BUTLER YEATS

Flowers are love's
truest language.

PARK BENJAMIN

*God writes the gospel
not in the Bible alone, but
on trees and flowers and
clouds and stars.*

MARTIN LUTHER

*Truths are first clouds; then
rain, then harvest and food.*

HENRY WARD BEECHER

*Enjoy your own life without
comparing it to another.*

MARQUIS DE CONDORCET

GOD DREAMED—THE SUNS SPRANG FLAMING INTO PLACE,
AND SAILING WORLDS WITH MANY A VENTUROUS RACE.
HE WOKE—HIS SMILE ALONE ILLUMINED SPACE.

AMBROSE BIERCE

Be inspired with the belief that life is a
great and noble calling; not a mean and
groveling thing that we are to shuffle through
as we can, but an elevated and lofty destiny.

WILLIAM E. GLADSTONE

I COUNT THIS THING TO BE
GRANDLY TRUE: THAT A NOBLE
DEED IS A STEP TOWARD GOD.

JOSIAH GILBERT HOLLAND

First keep the peace within yourself, then you can also bring peace to others.

THOMAS À KEMPIS

Always begin anew with
the day, just as nature does.

GEORGE WOODBERRY

WHATEVER IS RIGHT AND PURE

I t's one of those million-dollar mornings when you rise early without an alarm and feel refreshed. As you step out onto the front porch with a delicious cup of coffee, the light of dawn is just beginning to sparkle through the branches of the distant cedar trees. "Why don't I do this more often?" you ask the squirrel perched on the railing. He offers no comment but seems willing to remain and hear out your answer as you ease into the wicker chair.

A right and pure life merely requires a place to sit, an inspiring view, goodness to ponder, prayers of gratitude, and a gentle companion to talk to. The burdens we layer on top of this basic plan for good living are things that the squirrel couldn't care less about: car leases, job promotions, social networking, and the price of gas. These become, in time, the distractions that distance us from the purest, most sacred priorities for joy.

When dawn gives way to high noon and afternoon fades to dusk, you realize that you've barely moved. Your fulfilling day has consisted of meditating on God's splendor, retrieving a few coffee refills, and feeding mixed nuts from a glass candy dish to your new friend. As you stretch with satisfaction, you recall a childhood wish you had whispered to God one summer evening. You had wanted to become one of those rare grownups who delights in being alive. Now you realize this simple quest is more purposeful than an impressive resumé, more pure than perfection, and more wise than naive notions of "more is better." This is the night you go to bed knowing that prayers are answered.

God saw all that he had made, and it was very good.

GENESIS 1:31

Let every dawn of morning be to you as the beginning of life, and every setting sun be to you as its close, then let every one of these short lives leave its sure record of some kindly thing done for others, some goodly strength or knowledge gained for yourself.

JOHN RUSKIN

IT IS IN DEEP SOLITUDE THAT I FIND THE GENTLENESS WITH WHICH I CAN TRULY LOVE MY BROTHERS. THE MORE SOLITARY I AM THE MORE AFFECTION I HAVE FOR THEM.

THOMAS MERTON

There is one piece of advice, in a life of study, which I think no one will object to; and that is, every now and then to be completely idle—to do nothing at all.

SYDNEY SMITH

There is a pleasure in the pathless woods,
There is a rapture on the lonely shore,
There is society where none intrudes
By the deep sea, and music in its roar.

LORD GEORGE GORDON BYRON

I love the
silent hour
of night,
for blissful
dreams may
then arise,
revealing
to my
charmed
sight what
may not
bless my
waking
eyes.

ANNE BRONTË

TENSION IS WHO YOU
THINK YOU SHOULD
BE. RELAXATION IS
WHO YOU ARE.

CHINESE PROVERB

Keep yourself alive by throwing
day by day fresh currents of thought
and emotion into the things you
have come to do from habit.

JOHN LANCASTER SPALDING

Nothing is worth more than this day.

GOETHE

All mankind's troubles are
caused by one single thing,
which is their inability to sit
quietly in a room.

BLAISE PASCAL

There are certain half-dreaming moods of mind, in which we naturally steal away from noise and glare, and seek some quiet haunt, where we may indulge our reveries and build our air castles undisturbed.

WASHINGTON IRVING

YET THE FRESH AIR OF THE EVENING SIGHS AMONG THE LEAVES; THE BIRDS, THOSE VOICES OF THE FLOWERS, REPEAT THE EVENING PRAYER.

JEAN-BAPTISTE-CAMILLE COROT

Take delight in the LORD, and he will give you the desires of your heart.

PSALM 37:4

26

What sweet delight a quiet life affords.

William Drummond

WHATEVER IS LOVELY
AND ADMIRABLE

*I*n nature's living room, we can take in a majestic view of the endless space between ourselves and the setting sun or become enraptured by the miraculous details that seemingly multiply by the thousands as soon as we pay attention. The pointy nubs of a pinecone. The intricate veins in a single leaf. The spectrum of color in the sunset sky reflected on the lake.

These moments of external observation soon transition you back to internal discovery. Take in all that is lovely and admirable in your surroundings, your life, and in those friends, family, and mentors you cherish. Seeing the beauty of people, places, and experiences teaches you to recognize and appreciate the unique wonder of every moment.

Turn to the wisdom and insight found in tranquillity and think about who you admire in your life. The parent or grandparent who patiently taught you to bait a hook? Your child who bravely headed into the unknown land of kindergarten? Your friend who walks a narrow path of illness and still finds joy in the first buds of spring?

Stillness will serenade your life, and its lovely offering will rise at any moment and fill you with awe. Are you listening? Let beautiful melodies, words, and thoughts become your oxygen. Be filled.

This is the meeting place where God has set his bounds. Here is enough, at last, for eye and thought, restful and satisfying and illimitable. Here rest is sweet, and the picture of it goes with us on our homeward way, more lasting in memory than the sunset on the meadows or the lingering light across the silent stream.

ISAAC OGDEN RANKIN

The beauty of the world and the orderly arrangement of everything celestial make us confess that there is an excellent and eternal nature, which ought to be worshiped and admired by all mankind.

CICERO

HAPPINESS IS LIKE A BUTTERFLY WHICH, WHEN PURSUED, IS ALWAYS BEYOND OUR GRASP, BUT, IF YOU WILL SIT DOWN QUIETLY, MAY ALIGHT UPON YOU.

NATHANIEL HAWTHORNE

Climb the mountains and get their good tidings. Nature's peace will flow into you as sunshine flows into trees. The winds will blow their own freshness into you, and the storms their energy, while cares will drop away from you like the leaves of Autumn.

JOHN MUIR

In all things of

The LORD is good to all;
he has compassion on
all he has made.

PSALM 145:9

In nature there is something of the marvelous.

ARISTOTLE

Look to this day!
For it is life, the very life of life.
For yesterday is but a dream
And tomorrow is only a vision
But today well lived makes every
yesterday a dream of happiness
And tomorrow a vision of hope.
Look well, therefore, to this day!
Such is the salutation of the dawn.

KALIDASA

*True silence is the rest of
the mind; it is to the spirit
what sleep is to the body,
nourishment and refreshment.*

WILLIAM PENN

CHEERFULNESS KEEPS UP A KIND
OF DAYLIGHT IN THE MIND,
FILLING IT WITH A STEADY AND
PERPETUAL SERENITY.

JOSEPH ADDISON

How beautiful it is to do nothing

nd then to rest afterward. Spanish Proverb

WHATEVER IS EXCELLENT AND PRAISEWORTHY

*W*hen you are enveloped by nature's peace and strength, you feel the embrace of God. Silence allows you to become aware of all that is within you and around you. Once you shift your thoughts from worries to wonder and grumbles to gratitude, something remarkable happens—you receive clarity on the matters of importance and purpose that is beyond yourself.

The practice of praise will help you through times of discomfort, need, loss, want, and mediocrity. Celebrating all that is good and true and excellent gives you a mind-set of reverence. Seeking joy will elevate your heart's capacity for more love, more beauty, more compassion, and more abundant living.

Right now the moon is illuminating the trail to the lake. You feel the nudge. But unlike past times, you don't shrug away the longing. Instead, you start walking. You savor the intoxicating sweetness that infuses nightfall, and you put one foot in front of the other until you see it, a rope swing tied to an oak tree limb as high as heaven. It is the pendulum that transports the few, the brave, from the certainty of land to the ridiculously wonderful free fall before the splash. This time you see what is perfectly lovely about this moment. It was made for you. Go for it. Rejoice.

God is the friend of silence. See how nature—trees, flowers, grass—grows in silence; see the stars, the moon and the sun, how they move in silence... We need silence to be able to touch souls.

MOTHER TERESA

Happiness is like manna; it is to be gathered in grains, and enjoyed every day. It will not keep; it cannot be accumulated; nor have we got to go out of ourselves or into remote places to gather it since it is rained down from Heaven, at our very doors.

TRYON EDWARDS

THE PRAYER THAT BEGINS WITH THANKFULNESS, AND PASSES ON INTO WAITING, EVEN WHILE IN SORROW AND SORE NEED, WILL ALWAYS END IN THANKFULNESS, AND TRIUMPH, AND PRAISE.

ALEXANDER MACLAREN

It is tranquil people who accomplish much.

HENRY DAVID THOREAU

If the only prayer you said in your whole life was, "thank you," that would suffice.

MEISTER ECKHART

He is the word that speaks to us in the silences of the hills, and on the plains, and by the rivers. To listen is to be refreshed—is strength and peace.

Author unknown, *The Outlook* (May 4, 1901)

In all ranks of the life the human heart yearns for the beautiful; and the beautiful things that God makes are his gift to all alike.

Harriet Beecher Stowe

All the blessings of the fields,
All the stores the garden yields,
All the plenty summer pours,
Autumn's rich, o'erflowing stores...
Knowledge with its gladdening streams,
Pure religion's holier beams—
Lord, for these our souls shall raise
Grateful vows and solemn praise.

Sarah Hale

All God's pleasures are simple ones; the rapture of a May morning sunshine, the stream blue and green, kind words, benevolent acts, the glow of good humor.

F.W. Robertson

I go to nature to be soothed
and healed, and to have my
senses put in order.

JOHN BURROUGHS

SAYING THANK YOU IS MORE
THAN GOOD MANNERS. IT IS
GOOD SPIRITUALITY.

ALFRED PAINTER

Gratitude is the fairest blossom which springs from the soul.

HENRY WARD BEECHER

There is nothing that God hath established in a constant course of nature, and which therefore is done every day, but would seem a Miracle, and exercise our admiration, if it were done but once.

John Donne

Any one thing in the creation is sufficient to demonstrate a Providence to a humble and grateful mind.

Epictetus

When you drink the water, remember the spring.

Chinese Proverb

You Are Here

Wherever you go, there you are." This quote used to drive you nuts. It sounded like something an armchair sage offers up at a party when smooth pleasantries dwindle into itchy silence. But now? Now you hear it with ears that are in tune with the hum of a moonbeam, the laughter of flowers, and the joyful praises that resound in all of God's creation. You recognize that no matter where you go and no matter what you are experiencing, there is always an open invitation to follow the way to the heart of your heart.

See how far you've come? Your concern about being a visitor in a foreign land is replaced with confidence that you are right where you belong. Now you can deftly track a trail of thoughts that feed you, lead you, and precede a deep and lasting connection with the holy. You are opening the door to the home and truth of yourself. And as you enter the still and quiet place, the gentle breeze carries with it the most inviting, reassuring phrase you've ever heard—"Welcome home."

Your sacred space is where you can find yourself again and again.

JOSEPH CAMPBELL

43

To enjoy scenery you should ramble amidst it; let the feelings to which it gives rise mingle with other thoughts; look round upon it in intervals of reading; and not go to it as one goes to see the lions fed at a fair. The beautiful is not to be stared at, but to be lived with.

THOMAS BABINGTON MACAULAY

PEACE LIKE THE RIVER'S GENTLE FLOW,
PEACE LIKE THE MORNING'S SILENT GLOW,
FROM DAY TO DAY, IN LOVE SUPPLIED,
AN ENDLESS AND UNEBBING TIDE.

HORATIUS BONAR

Whatever enlarges hope will also exalt courage.

WILLIAM SAMUEL JOHNSON

A world without a Sabbath would be like a man without a smile, like a summer without flowers, and like a homestead without a garden.

HENRY WARD BEECHER

He enjoys true leisure who has time
to improve his soul's estate.

HENRY DAVID THOREAU

Take all the pleasures of all the spheres,
And multiply each through endless years,
One minute of Heaven is worth them all.

THOMAS MOORE

I try to avoid looking forward or

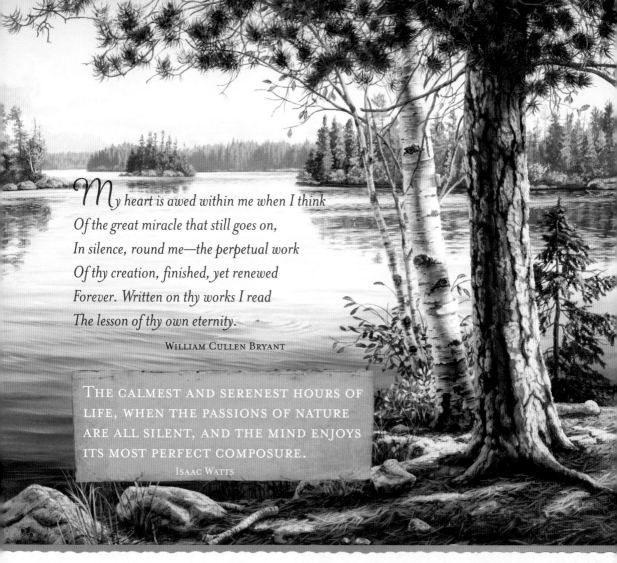

My heart is awed within me when I think
Of the great miracle that still goes on,
In silence, round me—the perpetual work
Of thy creation, finished, yet renewed
Forever. Written on thy works I read
The lesson of thy own eternity.

WILLIAM CULLEN BRYANT

THE CALMEST AND SERENEST HOURS OF
LIFE, WHEN THE PASSIONS OF NATURE
ARE ALL SILENT, AND THE MIND ENJOYS
ITS MOST PERFECT COMPOSURE.
ISAAC WATTS

backward, and try to keep looking upward.

CHARLOTTE BRONTË

To see a world in a grain of sand,

And a heaven in a wild flower,

Hold infinity in the palm of your hand,

An eternity in an hour.

WILLIAM BLAKE